A Visit to

The Farm

Revised Edition

by Blake A. Hoena

CAPSTONE PRESS
a capstone imprint

Pebble Plus is published by Capstone Press,
1710 Roe Crest Drive, North Mankato, Minnesota 56003
www.mycapstone.com

Library of Congress Cataloging-in-Publication Data
is available on the Library of Congress website.

ISBN 978-1-5435-0828-4 (library binding)
ISBN 978-1-5435-0840-6 (paperback)
ISBN 978-1-5435-0868-0 (ebook pdf)

Editorial Credits
Sarah Bennett, designer; Tracy Cummins, media researcher;
Laura Manthe, production specialist

Photo Credits
Alamy: Rafael Ben-Ari, 7; Capstone Press: Gary Sundermeyer,
Cover Background, 3, 5, 9, 13, 15, 17, 19; iStockphoto: mixetto,
21; Shutterstock: amirage, Design Element, Janis Apels, 11,
withGod, Cover Left

Note to Parents and Teachers

The A Visit to set supports national social studies standards
related to the production, distribution, and consumption of
goods and services. This book describes and illustrates a farm.
The images support early readers in understanding the text. The
repetition of words and phrases helps early readers learn new
words. This book also introduces early readers to subject-specific
vocabulary words, which are defined in the Glossary section.
Early readers may need assistance to read some words and to
use the Table of Contents, Glossary, Read More, Internet Sites,
Critical Thinking Questions, and Index sections of the book.

Table of Contents

The Farm

A farm is a fun place to visit.

Farms have buildings, fields,

and animals.

Farm Buildings

Barns are large buildings
where animals live.
Barns also hold crops
and equipment.
Farmers milk cows in barns.

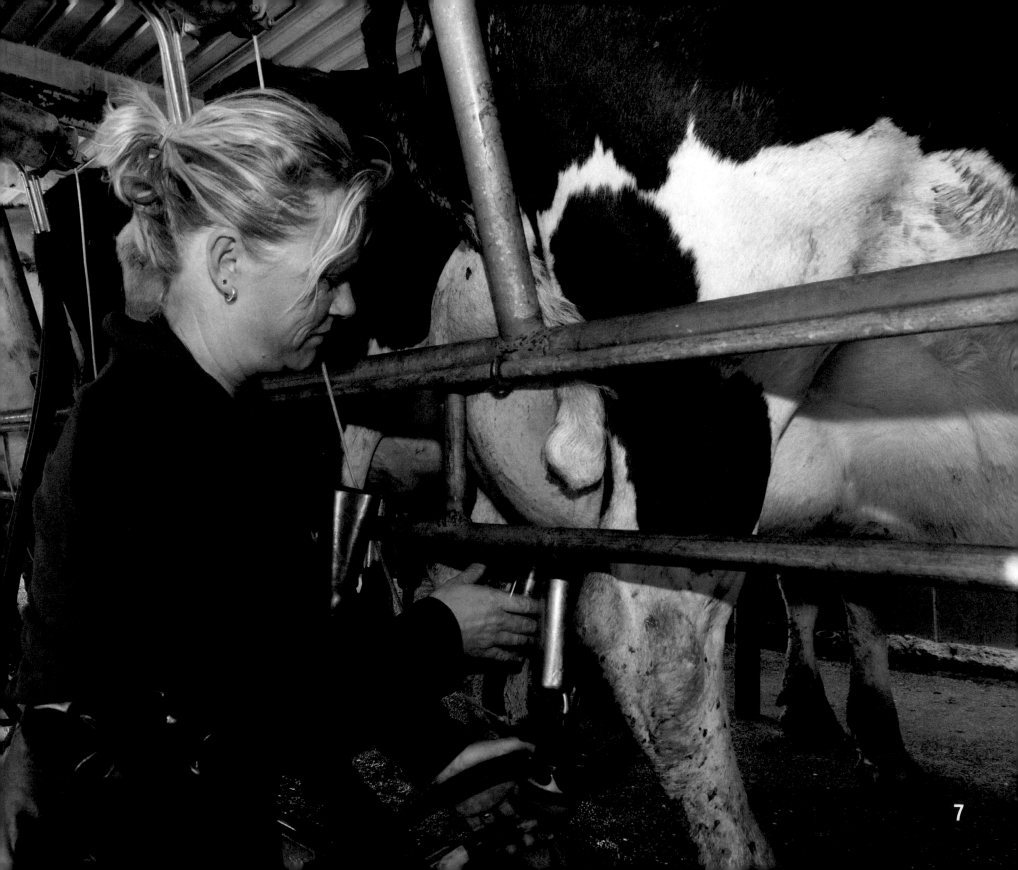

Bins hold food that

farm animals eat.

Bins are round and wide.

Farm Animals

Chickens look for food

around the farm.

They peck at the ground.

Sheep graze.

They eat the grass

in a pasture.

Pigs stay in their pens.

Pigs snort and squeal.

Fields and Crops

Farmers use tractors

in their fields.

Tractors pull

heavy machinery.

Farmers drive combines.

Combines help farmers pick

or harvest crops in the fall.

A farm is an important place.
The food people and animals eat
comes from a farm.

Glossary

barn—a building where animals, crops, and equipment are kept

combine—a powerful vehicle that picks or harvests crops when they are finished growing in a field

field—an area of land used for growing crops

graze—to eat grass that is growing in a field or pasture

pasture—the land that animals use to graze

tractor—a powerful vehicle that has large wheels; tractors pull farm machinery, hay wagons, and heavy loads

Read More

Cohn, Jessica. *On the Job at a Farm.* On the Job. South Egremont, Mass.: Red Chair Press, 2017.

Devera, Czeena. *Farmer.* My Friendly Neighborhood. Ann Arbor, Mich.: Cherry Lake Publishing, 2018.

Jeffries, Joyce. *Farmers.* Hands-on Jobs. New York: PowerKids Press, 2016.

Internet Sites

Use FactHound to find Internet sites related to this book.

Visit *www.facthound.com*

Just type **9781543508284** and go.

 Super-cool stuff! Check out projects, games and lots more at **www.capstonekids.com**

Critical Thinking Questions

1. Why are barns important on a farm?

2. Describe one or two jobs a farmer does on a farm.

3. Would you like to visit a farm? Why or why not?

Index